Such a Time as This

A General View of Bible Prophecy

Rosemary Hyslop

hysloprosemary@gmail.com
JesusAtoningLife.com

Editing, interior design and cover by Rachel L. Hall, Writely Divided Editing & More

Cover photo by Reijo Telaranta from Pixabay

Such a Time as This: A General View of Biblical Prophecy / Rosemary Hyslop. —1st edition.

ISBN: 979-8-9863533-5-7 Paperback
979-8-9863533-6-4 eBook

To those who seek
to understand
such a time as this

ESTHER 4:14

CONTENTS

PREFACE

PARENTS AND GRANDPARENTS often express great concern for their children's and grandchildren's futures as they wonder what kind of a world the next generations will face when they grow up. Yet, the time of one's birth is not accidental. We have each been born for "such a time as this" (Esther 4:14).

I have thought about how glad I am that my parents and grandparents did not have to face the kind of world I face. But they were not meant to face what I am facing. They were born for their time, not mine. So it is with our children. They have been born for their time. We can trust our loving God in all times and places.

Jesus told His disciples,

> *When they drag you into their meeting places, or into police courts and before judges, don't worry about defending yourselves—what you'll say or how you'll say it. The right words will be there.*

The Holy Spirit will give you the right words when the time comes.

Luke 12:12 MSG

Our faithful God is always ready for such a time as this. He desires that we also be ready, and He has provided His prophetic word for us so that we will be ready for such a time as this.

Rosemary Hyslop
Keystone Heights, Florida
September, 2023

Such a Time as This

THE TESTIMONY OF JESUS
IS THE SPIRIT OF PROPHECY

REVELATION 19:10 NASB

INTRODUCTION

WHEN WE THINK OF BIBLE PROPHECY, most of us think of the book of Revelation and the "end times." What are the end times? What is *ending*? Biblically, the end times precede the return of Jesus Christ to earth. His return ends the rule of Satan.

The Lord Jesus' message was, "Repent, for the kingdom of heaven is near" (Matthew 4:17 NET). He taught us to pray, "Your kingdom come your will be done on earth as it is in heaven" (Matthew 6:10 NASB). As God's kingdom comes, Satan's kingdom ends.

The casting out of Satan's kingdom will not be an easy task. One might think, "Since God is all-powerful, couldn't He have done it all in an easier way?" George MacDonald said, "All things are possible with God, but all things are not easy."*

---

* From MacDonald's "Life," in *Unspoken Sermons, Second Series* (Grand Rapids, MI: Christian Classics Ethereal Library), 64.

God has given His creation freedom. He does not make slaves or robots, nor does He want mere conformity to His laws. From the beginning, God's desire for humanity has been to make us in His image and likeness.

God is holy. Holiness is not only sinlessness; it is absolute righteousness. Holiness is a state of God's eternal Being. God cannot create holiness. He must give it by giving His own Life, which He did in the Incarnation, in the life and death of His only begotten Son.

Only as we receive God's divine Life can we become holy. The Incarnation took place not just to save us from our sins. We are saved from our sins because of the Incarnation. Being saved from our sins is just the introduction to God's great salvation (Hebrews 2:3).

"He has granted to us His precious and magnificent promises, in order that by them you might become partakers of the divine nature" (2 Peter 1:4 NASB). The magnificent promises that God gave to Israel were to give them a new heart and to put a new spirit within them (Ezekiel 36:26-27). This was realized after Jesus' ascension and the coming of the Holy Spirit at Pentecost.

God gave His Life *to humanity, not to angels*. Through humanity, the knowledge and righteousness of God is to permeate the entire creation so that no taint of evil can be found in the universe.

One of the Lord Jesus' kingdom parables expresses this: "The kingdom of heaven is like yeast that a woman mixed into a large amount of flour until the yeast worked its way through all the dough" (Matthew 13:33 GW).

God's plan for His creation is wonderful, glorious, and far above what we can imagine. Dare we question His wisdom in how best to accomplish it? Part of His plan includes suffering, and the Cross is at the heart of His creation.

As we consider the various revelations in the following chapters, it is helpful to keep in mind Jesus' words about the trials and tribulations to come. He calls them "birth pangs" (Matthew 24:8). When a mother gives birth, her labor pains become increasingly painful and frequent until the new life she carries bursts forth. The end of it all is life!

So, as we consider Bible prophecy and the judgments to come, may we see their meaning in the light of God's great and glorious plan for us and His whole creation.

PROPHECY

BEGINNING AT MOSES AND WITH ALL THE PROPHETS, HE EXPLAINED TO THEM THE THINGS CONCERNING HIMSELF IN ALL THE SCRIPTURES.

LUKE 24:27 NASB

PROPHECY IS MORE THAN TELLING THE FUTURE. It is the inspired declaration of divine will and purpose. The book of Revelation states that the testimony of Jesus is the spirit of prophecy (Revelation 19:10). Jesus both fulfills and reveals God's prophetic word. At the heart of Bible prophecy is a Person!

The revelation of Jesus opens up the meaning of the Bible, as the two disciples on the road to Emmaus found out (Luke 24:27). Later they said to one another, "Were not our hearts burning within us while He was speaking to us on the road, while He was explaining the Scriptures to us?" (Luke 24:32 NASB).

After the Holy Spirit anointed Jesus at His baptism, the Spirit led Jesus to meet Satan in the wilderness and face his testings. After Jesus fasted for 40 days and was very hungry, Satan suggested that Jesus turn the stones around him into bread to satisfy His hunger. Jesus answered Satan, "Man shall not live by bread alone, but by every word that proceeds from the mouth of God" (Matthew 4:4 NKJV). Later, angels ministered to Jesus, providing a lot more than bread.

Facts and figures are like bread that feeds the body. They satisfy the intellect. When studying the prophetic Word, we must look beyond the events themselves and find their meaning in the living Word, our Lord Jesus Christ.

THE SEALED SCROLL

LOOK, THE LION OF THE TRIBE OF JUDAH, THE ROOT OF DAVID, HAS CONQUERED; THUS HE CAN OPEN THE SCROLL AND ITS SEVEN SEALS.

REVELATION 5:5 NET

THE BOOK OF REVELATION BEGINS with this statement: "The revelation of Jesus Christ, which God gave Him."

In Revelation chapter 5, the Apostle John sees One seated on a throne holding a scroll, or book, in His right hand. The Amplified Bible states that the hand is open, indicating that the time has come for the scroll's contents to be revealed.

The scroll had writing on both the front and the back, the inside and the outside. No fact, no truth, nothing was missing or left out.

The scroll had seven seals, and seven is the number of completion or perfection. A seal on a document ensures its authenticity. Before the contents of a sealed document may be read, the seal must be broken. Only the one to whom the document is written may break the seal and read its contents.

At first, it looks like there is no one who can break the seals, open the book, and look into it. The Apostle John weeps bitterly about this. It is good when we want to know and understand the truth and what life is all about. We should share in the Apostle John's anguish until the One who is the Truth is revealed to us and in us.

But one of the 24 elders surrounding the throne said to John, "Stop weeping! Look, the Lion of the tribe of Judah, the root of David, has conquered; thus he can open the scroll and its seven seals" (Revelation 5:5 NET). The importance of Jesus' human heritage is emphasized here. He is from the tribe of Judah and of the root of David. The people called Jesus the "Son of David."

Then John "saw standing in the middle of the throne, and of the four living creatures, and in the middle of the elders, a Lamb that appeared to have been killed" (Revelation 5:6 NET).

Note the location of the Lamb. He is in the middle of the throne of God, the four living creatures, and the 24 elders. Jesus is at the very heart of God, creation, and humanity.

The Lamb appears to have been slain. The glorified Lord Jesus Christ, whom the Apostle John saw at the beginning of Revelation, proclaimed, "I was dead, and behold, I am alive forevermore, and I have the keys of death and of Hades" (Revelation 1:18 NASB).

Right before the Lord Jesus died, He cried out, "It is finished!" At that moment, He placed His signature as both Son of God and Son of Man on the scroll. He alone can break the seals and open the scroll because He is the fulfillment of all it contains. He is the eternal Word of God who wrote the book of God's creation (Proverbs 8:22-36)!

CONTENTS OF THE SCROLL

THEN I LOOKED, AND BEHOLD, A HAND WAS EXTENDED TO ME; AND LO, A SCROLL WAS IN IT. WHEN HE SPREAD IT OUT BEFORE ME, IT WAS WRITTEN ON THE FRONT AND BACK, AND WRITTEN ON IT WERE LAMENTATIONS, MOURNING AND WOE.

EZEKIEL 2:9–10 NASB

EZEKIEL'S SCROLL CORRESPONDS to the scroll in Revelation, which the Son took from the Father's hand. The contents of both scrolls contain "lamentations, mourning and woe." Such has been the history of this world.

The first four seals reveal the Four Horsemen of the Apocalypse. They are white, red, black, and pale, representing, respectively, forceful rule, war, famine, and death (Revelation 6:8).

The breaking of the first of the four seals reveals man's inhumanity to man in ruling over others through war, leading to all the horrors that war brings. The Lamb of God reveals the whole picture of human history, as He was a victim of the sin of humankind.

The breaking of the fifth seal reveals the souls of those martyred for their faithfulness to the Word of God. Ever since Cain murdered Abel, the righteous have been persecuted and slain by the unrighteous.

In some mysterious and wonderful way, the blood of those martyred for righteousness' sake shares in the virtue of Jesus' blood. The martyrs "were told to rest for a little longer, until the full number was reached of both their fellow servants and their brothers who were going to killed just as they had been" (Revelation 6:11 NET). The Apostle Paul wrote about the filling up of the sufferings of Christ (Colossians 1:24).

The suffering of all creatures is purposeful and is part of God's great plan. The Apostle Paul wrote to the church in Rome:

> *For I consider that the sufferings of this present time are not worthy to be compared with the glory that is to be revealed to us. For the anxious*

> *longing of the creation waits eagerly for the revealing of the sons of God. For the creation was subjected to futility, not willingly, but because of Him who subjected it, in hope that the creation itself also will be set free from its slavery to corruption into the freedom of the glory of the children of God. For we know that the whole creation groans and suffers the pains of childbirth together until now.*
>
> Romans 8:18–22 NASB

The breaking of the sixth seal reveals the Day of the Lord, a time of great upheaval when cataclysmic events will occur in the heavens as well as on earth. It is a time when the Lord and His holy angels disarm and destroy the strongholds of the evil one who has deceived the world down through the ages.

> *Blow a trumpet in Zion,*
> *And sound an alarm on My holy mountain!*
> *Let all the inhabitants of the land tremble,*
> *For the day of the LORD is coming;*
> *Surely it is near,*
> *A day of darkness and gloom,*
> *A day of clouds and thick darkness. ...*
> *...The earth quakes,*
> *The heavens tremble,*
> *The sun and the stars lose their brightness.*
> *The LORD utters His voice before His army;*
> *Surely His camp is very great,*
> *For strong is he who carries out His word.*

The day of the LORD is indeed great and very awesome,
And who can endure it?

Joel 2:1–2, 10–11 NASB

The whole world will be convicted of sin and the reality of the Living God.

Then the kings of the earth, the very important people, the generals, the rich, the powerful, and everyone, slave and free, hid themselves in the caves and among the rocks, "Fall on us and hide us from the face of the one who is seated on the throne and from the wrath of the Lamb, because the great day of their wrath has come, and who is able to withstand it?"

Revelation 6:15–17 NET

The Day of the Lord destroys all evil strongholds. The Truth must be faced by all. There is no escape (Hebrews 2:3).

As the wicked react, they do not just fear punishment. Consider what it is like when something evil you have done is exposed. Think of the shame of it. It is like being forcibly pushed out of a dark room into the light. Jesus said,

Everyone who does evil deeds hates the light and does not come to the light, so that their deeds will

> *not be exposed. But the one who practices the truth comes to the light, so that it may be plainly evident that his deeds have been done in God.*
>
> John 3:20–21 NET

The Day of the Lord will be a time of both spiritual and physical darkness. Cataclysms in the heavens will affect the sun, moon, and stars, diminishing their light. There will be a darkness like that described in Genesis 1:2 and at the Cross.

As Jesus was dying on the Cross, an inexplicable darkness descended. He cried out to God, "Why have you forsaken me?" In other words, "I am here. Why is the world dying? I am a part of this world." Before God and the whole creation, He proclaimed His faith in Himself as the Representative of humanity.

His cry of faith pierced the darkness. At that point, at three o'clock in the afternoon, the darkness lifted. The world was saved by the faith and faithfulness of the Man, Christ Jesus.

So it will be again when He returns. His light will overcome the darkness. The prophet Zechariah describes that Day:

> *When the Lord my God shall come and all the holy ones with Him, it shall come to pass that on that day there shall not be light; there shall be chill and cold during one day. That day is known*

> *to the Lord. It will neither be day nor night; but towards evening there will be light.*
>
> Zechariah 14:5–7 LXX

Jesus saves the day! Can you feel the spirit of that special evening? The final battle, Armageddon, is finished. There is a sense of peace that we feel when we watch a sunset. Jesus is now present, bringing the light of God's Life with Him!

When the seventh seal is broken, there is silence in heaven for half an hour. Silence suggests a great sense of holy reverence and awe regarding what is about to happen during the final judgments, which bring about the destruction of evil rule and authority and the establishment of everlasting righteousness.

Next, a golden censer is filled with incense mixed with the prayers of *all* the saints. We must not think of God's judgments as the expression of sinful, angry vengeance, which enjoys witnessing suffering. Even God's anger and vengeance are righteous expressions of His love for the world.

As we read about the horrendous events that take place during the trumpet and bowl judgments, we must remember that through them, God is allowing evil to take its natural course, just as He did when Jesus was arrested and crucified. But God, all the heavenly creatures, and all of the saints and their prayers are involved. God never loses control. God never ceases to be God! All that God does and allows is for the good of all.

THE COMING OF GOD'S KINGDOM

TELL US, WHEN WILL THESE THINGS HAPPEN? AND WHAT WILL BE THE SIGN OF YOUR COMING AND OF THE END OF THE AGE?

MATTHEW 24:3 NET

PROPHECY IS PRIMARILY ABOUT the coming of God's kingdom. Both John the Baptist and the Lord Jesus began their public ministries with the same message: "Repent, for the kingdom of heaven is at hand" (Matthew 3:2, 4:17 NASB). The Lord Jesus Christ is bringing the kingdom of God into the world, continuing God's work. He said, "My Father is working until now, and I too am working" (John 5:17 NET).

In the beginning, God created the heavens and the earth. How important this earth is! On earth, God created humankind. And on earth, God became flesh, a true human being. In Jesus, the Son, God became a part of His creation. He became what He had created!

"The true light, who gives light to everyone, was coming into the world" (John 1:9 NET). He *was coming*. He *came!* And He *is coming!* The bodily return of the Lord Jesus Christ to take His place as Ruler of all (Matthew 28:18) is at the heart of Bible prophecy.

When the Pharisees asked Jesus about the coming of the kingdom of God, Jesus answered, "The kingdom of God is in your midst" (Luke 17:21 NET). Jesus, a holy human being, is the realization of God's kingdom on earth. "For in him all the fullness of deity lives in bodily form" (Colossians 2:9 NET).

Before His Transfiguration, Jesus told His disciples that some of them would see the Son of Man coming in His kingdom (Matthew 16:28). What did those three disciples, Peter, James, and John, see? They saw the Son of Man glorified. His face shone like the sun and His clothing became white as light. The kingdom of God was coming in a glorified Man, God's Man!

Before His crucifixion, Jesus prayed to His heavenly Father, "Father glorify your name." The Father answered

His Son, "I have glorified it, and I will glorify it again" (John 12:28 NET). He did so by raising the Lord Jesus from the dead.

The coming of God's kingdom continues in all those who believe in God's Messiah and receive His Holy Spirit into their being. As the kingdom of God lives and grows within humanity, Satan's rule and kingdom are threatened. Thus, we have both physical and spiritual battles.

THE BATTLE BETWEEN GOOD AND EVIL

REMEMBER THE BATTLE.

JOB 41:8

THE SECOND VERSE OF GENESIS describes the earth as an empty, formless, dark place. "The earth was without form and void; and darkness was upon the face of the deep" (Genesis 1:2 KJV).

The Septuagint calls the deep the *abyss*. The Gap Theory suggests that there was a time gap between the first and second verses of Genesis, that something cataclysmic happened to make the world dark, without form and empty. We know God does not create formlessness, emptiness, and darkness: "God is light, and in him there is no darkness at all" (1 John 1:5 NET).

If there was a previous creation, God does not see fit to tell us about it. Perhaps it was a kingdom related to the principalities and powers in the heavenly places (Ephesians 6:12). Could Satan have ruled such a creation? We don't know, but something evil and dark caused what we see in Genesis 1:2. And that darkness entered the Garden of Eden in the form of a serpent.

But it is the present creation that concerns us, and humankind is its crown. The One through Whom all was created, the Logos (or Word) of God, became human flesh and blood on this earth. The earth is not some insignificant speck in God's universe. Earth is at the heart of God's creation. (It may be at the very center of the expanding universe!)

The Spirit of God began moving through the darkness over the face of the waters, or abyss, and He brought His light into the darkness. God said, "Let there be light, and there was light" (Genesis 1:3 NASB). God's next act was to separate the light from the darkness, and that separation has continued through the ages till today. We have light and dark, good and evil, life and death.

The Spirit of God progressively brings more and more light into our world, giving us a greater understanding of our Creator, His great plan for creation, and our place in it. The Gospel of John begins with a profound explanation of this process.

> *In the beginning was the Word, and the Word was with God, and the Word was fully God. The word was with God in the beginning. All things were created by him, and apart from him not one thing was created that has been created. In him was life, and the life was the light of mankind. And the light shines on in the darkness, but the darkness has not mastered it.*
>
> John 1:1–5 NET

The Life was the Light of mankind! The Son of God and Son of Man brings the Light of Life into the human race. A Man has become the Light-bearer and Life-giver of Almighty God! Jesus said, "I am the Light of the world; he who follows Me shall not walk in the darkness, but shall have the Light of life" (John 8:12 NASB).

In saving us from darkness, He had to walk through the darkness Himself. He entered the waters of the Jordan, confessing our sins as no other human being could. Then, He met our archenemy, Satan, right where he dwelt, in the wilderness, and refuted all of his temptations. Finally, on the Cross, He endured every arrow aimed at His holy humanity until Satan's quiver was empty, and evil could do no more than kill His body.

But the Father raised and glorified Jesus' holy body through the power of indestructible Life (Hebrews 7:16).

If Jesus won the battle, why does the evil one's reign continue? Just as Jesus learned obedience and was perfected through suffering (Hebrews 5:8 and 2:10), so must we.

God did not have to allow the Tree of the Knowledge of Good and Evil to be in the Garden of Eden, but He did. He could have prevented Eve from eating its fruit in disobedience to the Lord, but He didn't. We live in a world of free choice. We have the freedom to exercise our will, for good or bad. This world is full of trials, tribulations, and great suffering, but it is accomplishing wonderful things beyond what we could ask or think!

God allows the world to be as it is to give us the opportunity to exercise faith. The Lord Jesus Christ lived by faith. He wasn't a Superman who was playacting. His faith was genuine. Our religion is not magic. It is real! Sometimes we speak of faith casually. But faith is a great mystery. Faith comes from God. It is what links the human soul with the Being of Almighty God.

We find the definition of faith in Hebrews 11:1. It involves conviction and hope concerning things we cannot see with our physical eyes.

> *In hope we were saved. Now hope that is seen is not hope, because who hopes for what he sees? But if we hope for what we do not see, we eagerly wait for it with endurance.*
>
> Romans 8:24–25 NET

The exercise of faith is crucial to our spiritual stature. Faith enables God to make us in His own image and likeness.

A muscle develops strength through exercise and overcoming resistance.

> *Suffering produces endurance, and endurance, character, and character, hope. And hope does not disappoint, because the love of God has been poured out in our hearts through the Holy Spirit who was given to us.*
>
> Romans 5:3–5 NET

The reign of the evil one continues because God is not finished with this sinful world. The Apostle Paul calls it "the day of salvation" (2 Corinthians 6:2). This present world is like the womb where the new life is formed. Once birth takes place, what's there is there.

God has won the war, but those who believe – and those who do not – still have battles to face. We have the great privilege of participating in Jesus' victory.

Over 2,000 years have passed since the resurrection, and Satan continues to rule this world. He will do so until the true heir, the Lord Jesus Christ, returns to take His rightful place as ruler and head of humankind. His return is in process. The nearer He comes, the fiercer the battle.

Though we see suffering and chaos, we can be reassured God is ridding the world of evil. Wickedness cannot ultimately stand in the presence of the Holy One. Upon His return, the evil structure of Babylon will collapse.

BABYLON

ON HER FOREHEAD A NAME WAS WRITTEN, A MYSTERY, "BABYLON THE GREAT, THE MOTHER OF HARLOTS AND OF THE ABOMINATIONS OF THE EARTH."

REVELATION 17:5 NASB

APOSTATE RELIGION WAS FIRST ESTABLISHED AT BABEL, where the people built a city and a tower reaching into the heavens. Babel's tower was more than bricks. The people were searching and reaching for heavenly powers and knowledge, which was represented by Eden's Tree of the Knowledge of Good and Evil.

Instead of seeking to know the Lord, they sought to exalt themselves by gaining knowledge and power from evil beings in the heavenly places. The Apostle Paul warns us: “Our struggle is not against flesh and blood, but against the rulers, against the powers, against the world rulers of this darkness, against the spiritual forces of evil in the heavens” (Ephesians 6:12 NET).

The primeval struggle between light and darkness, truth and lies, righteousness and wickedness, life and death, has continued throughout the millennia. The closer we come to the return of Jesus Christ, the division between good and evil will become more pronounced, and the power of the enemy will increase (Matthew 24:12). But we must not lose faith because “as sin reigned in death, so also grace will reign through righteousness to eternal life through Jesus Christ our Lord” (Romans 5:21 NET).

The prophet Zechariah gives an interesting prophetic vision of the course of evil during the end times (Zechariah 5). Evil is swept away, gathered together, and carried to its final end. The Lord will send a curse to enter every house where evil is found. A measuring basket will go forth containing a woman called Wickedness. She is thrown down into the bottom of the basket and a lead lid is closed over her. Two vultures transport the basket to the Land of Shinar or Babylonia. Wickedness, measured and contained, will be placed on its own base there in the place where organized godlessness began and where it will end.

Ancient Babylon will likely be restored in the latter days. Zechariah's prophecy suggests this location (Zechariah 5:11). The area lies about 55 miles south of modern Baghdad.

Interestingly, Saddam Hussein began restoring the city of ancient Babylon. The Middle East has become extremely prosperous. The world's highest towers are found there. They speak of economic prosperity. Money, whether it be the dollar, the euro, or the dinar, is worshiped by a godless society. Paul warned: "For the love of money is the root of all evil" (1 Timothy 6:10 KJV).

Whoever controls the money *controls.* During the reign of the Antichrist, one will not be able to buy or sell without the Mark of the Beast (Revelation 13:17).

End time Babylon will be the hub of world trade. Revelation 18:13 lists the items of world trade, which include human lives, their bodies and souls. Today, second only to drug trafficking, human trafficking is the fastest-growing criminal industry in the world.*

Most of humanity alive at the time of the trumpet and bowl judgments will refuse to repent:

---

* Ewelina U. Ochab, "The World's Fastest Growing Crime." Forbes. July 29, 2017. https://www.forbes.com/sites/ewelinaochab/2017/07/29/the-worlds-fastest-growing-crime/?sh=2d2a6e43aae1.

> *The rest of humanity, who had not been killed by these plagues, did not repent of the works of their hands, so that they did not stop worshiping demons and idols made of gold, silver, bronze, stone, and wood – idols that cannot see or hear or walk about. Furthermore, they did not repent of their murders, of their magic spells, of their sexual immorality, or of their stealing.*
>
> Revelation 9:20–21 NET

Note that stealing is listed with murder, demonism, and sexual immorality. The 8th commandment is "You shall not steal." Stealing is taking from another that which is not yours.

Totalitarianism is a form of government established on stealing, taking from the individual and giving to a select few who think they know what you should have and what you should do with it. The final One World Order under the Antichrist will be the epitome of totalitarian rule.

Babylon is both a corrupt economic/political system and an unclean religious system. In most pagan religions, a female figure, a goddess of love and fertility, is worshiped. She has been given many names, some of which are Astarte, Ishtar, Asherah, Artemis, Diana, Aphrodite, Venus, Isis, and the Queen of Heaven.

Idolatry leads to demonism and all kinds of sexually unclean practices. The Harlot of Babylon "held in her hand a golden cup filled with detestable things and unclean things from her sexual immorality" (Revelation 17:4 NET).

Eventually, the Beast turns on the Harlot, which represents apostate religion, and destroys her. Godless totalitarianism will use religion as long as religion conforms to its will and serves its purpose. Once religion is no longer needed by the world's economic/political system, the apostate church will be destroyed by the Beast on which the Harlot rides (Revelation 17:16).

Western civilization has known the blessings and freedom that come from knowing God's Word and respecting His laws. As societies drift away from God, people will become increasingly insensitive to what is right and good. As they become corrupt and degenerate, they will bring about the decay of Judeo-Christian civilization. The internal evils of Babylon are self-destructive.

> *Fallen, fallen is Babylon the great! She has become a dwelling place of demons and a prison of every unclean spirit, and a prison of every unclean and hateful bird. For the nations have drunk of the wine of the passion of her immorality, and the kings of the earth have committed acts of immorality with her, and the merchants of the earth have become rich by the wealth of her sensuality.*
>
> Revelation 18:2–3 NASB

The city of Babylon will be judged in one hour. When the seventh bowl is poured out, the greatest earthquake ever will occur. Islands will disappear, mountains will be flattened, and huge hailstones weighing about 100 pounds each will fall from heaven (Revelation 16:17–21).

Most of God's judgments come about by God simply withdrawing His protection. Chapter one of Romans states three times that God "gave them over" or *allowed* them. And God takes responsibility for all He allows.

Sinful humanity, under the rule of Satan, brings upon itself most of the suffering, destruction, and death that has taken place throughout human history. The first of the Four Horsemen of Revelation, the rider of the white horse, goes out conquering and to conquer (Revelation 6:2). Satan is the Destroyer. It is he and those who follow his rule who bring about destruction and death.

Babylon will reach its pinnacle under the reign of the Beast. The Tower of Babel will finally be completed. God put a stop to the building of the first tower, but during the end time, He will allow evil to run its full course. Then, with the return of the Lord Jesus Christ, the Tower of Babel will collapse, never to rise again!

DANIEL'S 70 WEEKS

SEVENTY SETS OF SEVEN TIME PERIODS HAVE BEEN ASSIGNED FOR YOUR PEOPLE AND YOUR HOLY CITY. THESE TIME PERIODS WILL SERVE TO BRING AN END TO REBELLION, TO STOP SIN, TO FORGIVE WRONGS, TO USHER IN EVERLASTING RIGHTEOUSNESS, TO PUT A SEAL ON A PROPHET'S VISION, AND TO ANOINT THE MOST HOLY ONE.

DANIEL 9:24 GW

THE BOOK OF DANIEL WAS WRITTEN IN BABYLON during the 70-year Babylonian captivity of Judah. Isn't it interesting that God gave Daniel this great prophecy while he was a captive in Babylon?

Chapter nine of Daniel has one of the most important prophecies in the Bible, the Seventy Weeks prophecy, each week representing a period of seven years, a week of years. Verses 24-27 summarize a period of time during which God accomplishes His greatest work through the nation of Israel. Israel and Jerusalem are central to the meaning of world history and God's eternal purpose for humankind.

All of Israel's previous history was a preparation for Daniel's 70 weeks. The 70 weeks of years begins long after God called Abraham, Isaac, and Jacob.

Through Jacob's trials, as he struggled with God and man, God finally gave him the name *Israel,* a name of great importance. Jacob's twelve sons became twelve tribes. Through the furnace of their captivity in Egypt, which lasted for 400 years, the twelve tribes of Israel became a nation. Then God gave Israel Moses, who led them out of Egypt and gave them God's Law. The infant nation was tested and tried during 40 years of wandering in the wilderness. Even after they reached the Land of Promise, they fought and struggled with the pagan nations around them, adopting their idolatrous ways.

Not until their 70-year captivity in Babylon, where idolatry was first established, did they get delivered from idolatry. Only a remnant returned from Babylon to the land God had given them, but God used that remnant to begin His greatest work through the Jewish nation. God was ready, and the little nation of Israel was ready.

Seventy weeks of years is a total of 490 years. The 490 years are separated into three periods: 7 weeks, 62 weeks, and one week. The first 7 weeks, or 49 years, start at the end of the Babylonian captivity. They cover the restoration of Jerusalem, repair of the wall, and rebuilding of the temple which Nebuchadnezzar had destroyed. The books of Ezra and Nehemiah give the history of that period.

The next 62 weeks, or 434 years, cover the time up to the crucifixion of Jesus. The Septuagint states, "After the sixty-two weeks, the Messiah shall be cut off, though there is no crime in him" (Daniel 9:26 LXX).

Just forty years after Messiah was cut off, the Roman general Titus destroyed the Jewish temple and Jerusalem. The Jews were scattered, and the Christian age began.

The present Christian age is like a parentheses, a period interrupting Israel's 70 weeks of years. The events of those final seven years, Daniel's 70th Week, will primarily concern the nation of Israel and the Jews.

In Daniel's prophecy, the city and the sanctuary will be destroyed by the people of the prince who is to come (Daniel 9:26). Titus, the one who destroyed Jerusalem and the temple, was a Roman general. Many Christian scholars believe that the *prince to come* will be the Antichrist. If this is true, the coming Antichrist will come out of the Roman Empire.

But isn't the Roman Empire past history? Not necessarily. Prophetic scholars have suggested that the present-day European Union (EU) is a revival of the Roman Empire, and even the United States, which grew out of Britain and Europe, can be considered as part of a revived Roman Empire. Rome's symbol of authority was the eagle. Perhaps not coincidentally, the United States' emblem is the bald eagle.

Rome brought civilization to Europe. The EU grew out of the EEC, the European Economic Community. The EEC was established in Rome in 1957 by the Treaty of Rome. The EEC became the EU in 1993. Since then, the EU has become increasingly significant on the world scene.

Daniel's prophecy states there will be war, destruction, and desolations until the end (Daniel 9:26). History has been filled with wars between nations, culminating in the First and Second World Wars. To this very day, we are faced with the threat of a third world war.

The prince who is to come will make a covenant with many for one week (Daniel 9:27). If the *prince to come* is the Antichrist and out of Rome, we could expect he will come from the revived Roman Empire. Will it be Germany again? The archeological remains of Satan's throne (Revelation 2:13) were removed from Pergamum in the late 1800s and are currently in Berlin's Pergamum Museum.

History records many peace treaties between nations, but keep in mind Daniel's covenant concerns the Jews and the nation of Israel. Many believe that Daniel's 70th week will begin with the signing of a peace treaty between Israel and other nations.

On September 15, 2020, on the South Lawn of the White House, Israel, the United Arab Emirates, and Bahrain signed the Abraham Accords, recognizing Israel's sovereignty. This "Treaty of Peace" or "Declaration of Peace" was negotiated by the United States' President Trump. Since then, other countries have joined the Accords in one way or another. The Abraham Accords are a preview of the coming great peace treaty when the world will again be fooled, as it was in 1938 when British Prime Minister Neville Chamberlain signed the Munich Agreement to appease Hitler. The hope was "Peace for our time."

Once Daniel's 70th week begins, many will believe that a lasting world peace has finally been accomplished. But when they say, "Peace, peace," then comes sudden destruction (1 Thessalonians 5:3)!

Daniel prophesied,

> *He will confirm a covenant with many for one week. But in the middle of that week he will bring sacrifices and offerings to a halt. On the wing of abominations will come one who destroys, until the decreed end is poured out on the one who destroys.*
>
> Daniel 9:27 NET

Israel will be deceived. "They have healed the brokenness of My people superficially, saying, 'Peace, peace,' but there is no peace. Were they ashamed because of the abomination they have done" (Jeremiah 6:14-15 NASB).

The Antichrist will bring about the "abomination that makes desolate" (Matthew 24:15). He will break the covenant in the middle of the 70th week, which will be followed by the Great Tribulation and Jacob's Trouble, the greatest persecution of the Jews, ever.

We can surmise that the "peacemaker" will be well-liked and attractive. Since he will be Satan's man, he will have all of the deceit and power of Satan. "By his treachery he will succeed through deceit. He will have an arrogant attitude, and he will destroy many who are unaware of his schemes" (Daniel 8:25 NET).

In the middle of the 70th week, Antichrist enters Israel's temple and sets himself up as God. This will be Satan's D-Day. Remember his words to Eve in the Garden of Eden? "You shall be as God."

Satan promised to give Jesus all the kingdoms of the world and their glory if Jesus would worship him (Matthew 4:8-9). Satan could not deceive Jesus, but he will be successful with many who lust for power and want control over nations. Receiving his power from Satan, the Antichrist and his followers will do the bidding of Satan.

Another name for Satan is "Destroyer." Revelation 9:11 states that the king of the abyss has the name *Abaddon* (Hebrew) or *Apollyon* (Greek), meaning "destruction." The king of the abyss is Satan, a fallen angel.

Satan covets the place God has given humanity in His Son; therefore, Satan hates humanity and desires total destruction of the human race. Little do those serving him know that he does not like them any more than he likes Jews or Christians. They are but his puppets–good for only however long he can use them. The Lord Jesus' return saves the human race and the earth from total destruction.

Daniel summarizes in one verse all that is to be accomplished in 70 weeks of years.

> *Seventy weeks are determined*
> *For your people and for your holy city,*
> *To finish the transgression,*
> *To make an end of sins,*
> *To make reconciliation for iniquity,*
> *To bring in everlasting righteousness,*
> *To seal up vision and prophecy,*
> *And to anoint the Most Holy.*
>
> Daniel 9:24 NKJV

Sin is done away with: it is expiated and atoned for. Reconciliation between God and man is realized, righteousness is established forever, all prophecy is fulfilled, and the Most Holy is anointed. Israel's 70 weeks finalizes "vision and prophecy."

THE OLIVET DISCOURSE

See MATTHEW 24, MARK 13, LUKE 21

THE LOCATION OF THE BODILY RETURN of the Lord Jesus Christ will be the Mount of Olives, from where He ascended into heaven (Acts 1:14). "In that day His feet will stand on the Mount of Olives, which is in front of Jerusalem on the east" (Zechariah 14:4 NASB). It is fitting that Jesus delivered His prophetic discourse from the Mount of Olives.

As Jesus spoke of the events preceding His return, He probably had the Eastern Gate in view. When He returns to earth, He will cross the Kidron Valley from the Mount of Olives and enter Jerusalem through the Eastern Gate.

Jesus' disciples had been admiring the magnificence of the temple. Jesus' shocking response awakened their interest regarding end-time events. His answer to them was, "As for these things which you are looking at, the days will come in which there will not be left one stone upon another which will not be torn down" (Luke 21:6 NASB). And 40 years after His crucifixion, the Jewish temple was destroyed by the Roman governor, Titus.

Jesus begins the Olivet Discourse by warning the disciples to not be deceived, that many would come in His name saying that they are the Christ (anointed one) and would deceive many. Today, self-proclaimed prophets claim to be anointed by God, to have special insight into what will happen and when. However, Jesus declared, "Of that day and hour no one knows, not even the angels in heaven, nor the Son, but only the Father" (Mark 13:32 NKJV).

He goes on to say that there will be "wars and rumors of wars," and nations and kingdoms will rise up against each other. There will be great earthquakes, plagues, and famines. Jesus called these "birth pangs." He cautioned the disciples, saying, "The end is not yet" (Matthew 24:6-8). But as birth nears, labor pains become more frequent and painful. So will be the nature of events preceding the return of Jesus Christ.

Jesus warns His disciples about the coming persecution. "They will deliver you up to tribulation and kill you, and you will be hated by all nations for My name's sake" (Matthew 24:9 NKJV). Both Jews and Christians have been persecuted throughout history. Even Christians themselves have persecuted both Jews and other Christians. Unfortunately, the Church does not escape the influence of Satan and is not immune to his schemes.

During the Holocaust, the earthly Church and many Christians turned their backs on the Jews. Fear of Hitler and his henchmen was a big factor. Those who would gain control over other human beings use fear. But the Christian persecution of Jews throughout history is devilish and inexplicable. It is inspired by Satan. Its root is not human!

The end times will bring apostasy, falling away from the truth, lawlessness, and lovelessness. We are forewarned that "brother will deliver brother to death, and a father his child; and children will rise up against parents and have them put to death" (Mark 13:12 NASB).

The Abomination of Desolation will stand in the holy place, and armies will surround Jerusalem. "For then there will be great tribulation, such as has not occurred since the beginning of the world until now, no, nor ever shall. ... False christs and false prophets will rise and show great signs and wonders to deceive, if possible, even the elect" (Matthew 24:21, 24 NASB). Yet, amid all this, the gospel of the kingdom will be preached to the whole world as a witness to all the nations.

After the Great Tribulation, cosmic events will take place:

> *Immediately after the tribulation of those days the sun will be darkened, and the moon will not give its light, and the stars will fall from the sky, and the powers of heavens will be shaken. Then the sign of the Son of Man will appear in the sky, and then all the tribes of the earth will mourn ... and they will see the Son of Man coming on the clouds of heaven with power and great glory.... And He will send out His angels with a loud trumpet call, and they will gather His elect from the four winds, from one end of the universe to the other.*
>
> Matthew 24:29–31 AMPC

The days of the coming of the Son of Man will be like the days of Noah. It will be sudden and unexpected.

> *As the days of Noah were, so also will the coming of the Son of Man be. For as in the days before the flood, they were eating and drinking, marrying and giving in marriage, until the day that Noah entered the ark, and did not know until the flood came and took them all away, so also will the coming of the Son of Man be. Then two men will be in the field; one will be taken and the other left. Two women will be grinding at the mill: one will be taken and the other left. Watch therefore,*

for you do not know what hour your Lord is coming.

Matthew 24:38–42 NKJV

Jesus concludes His Olivet Discourse with warnings to His followers. "Watch out! Stay alert! For you do not know when the time will come" (Mark 13:32 NET).

THE TIMES OF THE GENTILES

JERUSALEM WILL BE TRAMPLED DOWN BY THE GENTILES UNTIL THE TIMES OF THE GENTILES ARE FULFILLED.

LUKE 21:24 NET

CHRISTIAN HISTORY WOULD HAVE BEEN VERY DIFFERENT if the Jewish nation had repented after Jesus' ascension and the coming of the Holy Spirit at Pentecost. The Apostle Peter said,

> *Repent therefore and return, that your sins may be wiped away, in order that times of refreshing may come from the presence of the Lord; and that He may send Jesus, the Christ appointed for you, whom heaven must receive until the period of restoration of all things about which God spoke*

> *by the mouth of His holy prophets from ancient time.*
>
> Acts 3:19–21 NASB

But the Jewish leaders in Judea and in the Gentile nations where they were scattered did not repent. While many Jews believed in Jesus as Messiah, their leaders rejected Him and stirred up both Jews and Gentiles to persecute the Apostle Paul and those with him who proclaimed Jesus.

The Jews' "partial hardening," as Paul describes it, opened the way for the ingathering of the Gentiles. "I do not want you to be ignorant of this mystery, brothers and sisters, so that you may not be conceited: A partial hardening has happened to Israel until the full number of the Gentiles has come in" (Romans 11:25 NET).

Before His crucifixion, Jesus said to His people, the Jews, "I say to you, from now on you shall not see Me until you say, 'Blessed is He who comes in the name of the Lord'" (Matthew 23:39 NASB). He was quoting Psalm 118:26, which prophesies the Messiah's return to and fight for Israel. In that Day, every Jew will say, "Blessed is He who comes in the name of the Lord," and all Israel shall be saved (Romans 11:26).

God told Abraham that through his seed, all the nations of the earth would be blessed (Genesis 22:18). It was through the nation of Israel that God brought forth His Son, who is the Savior of the world, of both Jews and Gentiles.

> *From the standpoint of the gospel they are enemies for your sake, but from the standpoint of God's choice they are beloved for the sake of the fathers; for the gifts and the calling of God are irrevocable. For just as you once were disobedient to God, but now have been shown mercy because of their disobedience, so these also now have been disobedient, that because of the mercy shown to you they also may now be shown mercy. For God has shut up all in disobedience so that He may show mercy to all.*
>
> Romans 11:28–32 NASB

We can never fathom the depth of God's wisdom. His sovereign will is intricately woven into mankind's freedom.

An outstanding example of this truth is what happened to Joseph and his brothers. Out of jealousy, his brothers sell Joseph to Egypt. Years later, due to a great famine, Joseph's brothers leave their home to go to Egypt to buy grain. Eventually, his brothers recognize Joseph, who had become a highly-ranked official to Pharaoh. Joseph's words to them are classic. "You meant evil against me, but God meant it for good in order to bring about this present result, to preserve many people alive" (Genesis 50:20 NASB).

How nearsighted we all are, Jew and Gentile, failing to see the forest for the trees. God chose Abraham, Isaac, Jacob, and their descendants to carry, preserve, and bring forth His holy Seed into the world. "In your seed all the nations of the earth shall be blessed" (Genesis 22:18 NASB). The promised Seed of the woman is our Lord Jesus Christ.

Moses warned Israel that God would raise up from among them one who would speak God's word to them, and they should listen to him (Deuteronomy 18:15-19). But Israel's leaders rejected the Lord Jesus, their Messiah.

Paul warns the Church to not become proud of its present blessed position in God's plan.

> *If some of the branches were broken off, and you being a wild olive, were grafted in among them and became partaker with them of the rich root of the olive tree, do not be arrogant toward the branches; but if you are arrogant, remember that it is not you who supports the root, but the root supports you. You will say then, "Branches were broken off so that I might be grafted in." Quite right, they were broken off for their unbelief, but you stand by your faith. Do not be conceited, but fear; for if God did not spare the natural branches, He will not spare you, either.*
>
> Romans 11:17–21 NASB

A sign of the times is the growing acceptance of Replacement theology, which says the Christian Church has replaced Israel and that God has rejected Israel. But the gifts and calling of God are irrevocable (Romans 11:29). Nothing can change God's calling and promises to Israel (or Jacob)! Israel is the Church's root. If you cut off the root of a plant, it dies. Replacement theology is Satanic. It supports Satan's hatred for the Jews and the nation of Israel and is a cardinal sign of the growing apostasy of the Church.

THE GREAT APOSTASY

FALSE CHRISTS AND FALSE PROPHETS WILL ARISE AND WILL SHOW GREAT SIGNS AND WONDERS, SO AS TO MISLEAD, IF POSSIBLE, EVEN THE ELECT.

MATTHEW 24:24 NASB

THE BIBLE STATES THAT DURING THE END TIME, the Church will become apostate, deny the truth of God, and have the form of religion but deny its power.

> *Understand this, that in the last days difficult times will come. For people will be lovers of themselves, lovers of money, boastful, arrogant, blasphemers, disobedient to parents, ungrateful, unholy, unloving, irreconcilable, slanderers, without self–control, savage, opposed to what is good, treacherous, reckless, conceited, loving pleasure rather than loving God. They will*

> *maintain the outward appearance of religion but will have repudiated its power.*
>
> 2 Timothy 3:1–5 NET

In the book of Revelation, the last of the seven letters to the churches is to the church of Laodicea (Revelation 3:14-22). The Lord tells them they are neither hot nor cold and that while they think they are rich and in need of nothing, they are poor, blind, and naked.

The Apostle Paul wrote to Timothy,

> *For the time will come when they will not endure sound doctrine; but wanting to have their ears tickled, they will accumulate for themselves teachers in accordance to their own desires, and will turn away their ears from the truth and will turn aside to myths.*
>
> 2 Timothy 4:3–4 NASB

The Day of the Lord will not come until the rebellion and apostasy of the Church takes place and the Antichrist is revealed.

> *Now in regard to the coming of our Lord Jesus Christ and our gathering together to meet Him, we ask you, brothers and sisters, not to be quickly unsettled or alarmed either by a so–called prophetic revelation of a spirit or a message or a letter alleged to be from us, to the effect that the day of the Lord has already come. Let no one in any way deceive or entrap you, for*

> *that day will not come unless the apostasy comes first, that is, the great rebellion, the abandonment of the faith by professed Christians, and the man of lawlessness is revealed, the son of destruction, the Antichrist, the one who is destined to be destroyed, who opposes and exalts himself, so proudly and so insolently, above every so-called god or object of worship, so that he actually enters and takes his seat in the temple of God, publicly proclaiming that he himself is God.*
>
> 2 Thessalonians 2:1–4 AMP

Rebellion and lawlessness go together. The Church becomes apostate as its members reject the truths of the Bible and presume to do their own thing, as it was in Israel's days of the judges. Everyone did what was right in their own eyes (Judges 21:25). The apostate Church opens the way for the reign of the Lawless one, the Antichrist.

As we see Christian civilization, particularly in the United States of America, becoming increasingly godless, we also see the fulfillment of prophecies regarding the nation of Israel.

With the apostasy of the Church, Israel will become the primary focus of the Holy Spirit's ministry. In the late 19th century, Theodor Herzl's vision of a homeland for Jews began to take shape as Zionism. Then in 1917, the British government made the Balfour Declaration, supporting the establishment of a homeland for Jews in what was then called Palestine and is now the nation of Israel.

Israel's restoration as a nation in 1948 is a miracle, a fulfillment of God's promise to the Jews. The following are just a few of the many prophecies promising the restoration of Israel:

> *Hear the word of the LORD, O nations,*
> *And declare in the coastlands afar off,*
> *And say, 'He who scattered Israel will gather him*
> *And keep him as a shepherd keeps his flock.'*
>
> Jeremiah 31:10 NASB

> *For a brief moment I forsook you,*
> *But with great compassion I will gather you.*
>
> Isaiah 54:7 NASB

> *"Then they will know that I am the LORD their God because I made them go into exile among the nations, and then gathered them again to their own land; and I will leave none of them there any longer. I will not hide My face from them any longer, for I will have poured out My Spirit on the house of Israel," declares the Lord GOD.*
>
> Ezekiel 39: 28–29 NASB

The writer to the Hebrews, in the chapter of the faithful under the old covenant, concludes with this statement: "And all these, having obtained a good testimony through faith, did not receive the promise, God having provided something better for us, that they should not be made perfect apart from us" (Hebrews 11:39-40 NKJV). Israel's great blessing waits for the ingathering of the Gentiles. Israel and the Church are intricately entwined.

When Israel rejected God's Promise of the Holy Spirit (Ezekiel 36:26-27), the Gentiles received it. Because of Israel's rejection, the Gentiles have been brought in. But the day is coming when Israel will be restored. "If the casting away of them be the reconciling of the world, what shall the receiving of them be, but life from the dead" (Romans 11:15 KJV). We can't even imagine what all that will entail.

But first, evil must run its course – the great apostasy, the coming of the Antichrist, the Great Tribulation, Jacob's Trouble, judgment on Babylon, the Battle of Armageddon, the bodily return of the Lord Jesus Christ and the judgment of the Beast and Satan.

SPIRIT OF ANTICHRIST

BY THIS YOU KNOW THE SPIRIT OF GOD: EVERY SPIRIT THAT CONFESSES THAT JESUS CHRIST HAS COME IN THE FLESH IS OF GOD, AND EVERY SPIRIT THAT DOES NOT CONFESS THAT JESUS CHRIST HAS COME IN THE FLESH IS NOT OF GOD. AND THIS IS THE SPIRIT OF THE ANTICHRIST.

1 JOHN 4:3 NKJV

The Great Apostasy of the Church ushers in the reign of Satan's man, the Antichrist, also called the lawless one, the man of sin.

The Apostle John states that the spirit of the Antichrist is a denial of the Incarnation. We hear a lot about the coming Antichrist but little about the *spirit* of Antichrist.

John also says that there have been many antichrists (1 John 2:18).

It is the spirit of Antichrist that brings about the apostasy of the Church and the revealing of a great personage who will embody the rebellion of the Church and the spirit of Antichrist.

I heard a Christian scholar of the prophetic scriptures say that he believed that Satan had "his man" in the wings for every generation. What holds Satan back? The Spirit of God does.

> *For the hidden power of lawlessness is already at work. However, the one who holds him back will do so until he is taken out of the way, and then the lawless one will be revealed.*
>
> 2 Thessalonians 2:7–8 NET

Years ago, I watched a TV interview of one of Hitler's military leaders. At the time of the interview, the man was old. He spoke in German, which was translated. He visited Hitler in his underground bunker in Berlin. He wanted to die with Hitler, but Hitler told him that it was not necessary and that he should leave the bunker and go his way. He asked Hitler, "My Führer, where shall I go?" Hitler got a faraway look in his eyes and said, "Wait for the coming man!"

How is the spirit of Antichrist the denial that Jesus Christ has come in the flesh? The better we understand the spirit or motivation behind something, the better will we understand what really is going on.

When Satan told Eve that she could be like God if she would just step out on her own, so to speak, and do her own thing apart from the will of God, Satan was sowing the seed of the spirit of Antichrist. We could call it the seed of Satan.

The "seed of the woman" is the Lord Jesus Christ. When God entrusted His eternal Son to humanity in the womb of the Virgin Mary, that holy Gift to us proclaimed the place that God has given to the human race.

Satan is an angel – a fallen one, but still an angelic being. Why did he attack God's human creation in Eden? Because he hoped to ruin us for God. He wanted the place that God was giving to humanity through His Son.

Hebrews chapter 2 explains humanity's high calling, that it was not to angels that God has subjected the world to come but to humankind through Jesus, who is both Son of God and Son of Man.

If we look closely at the nature of the temptations Satan presented to Jesus, we see how Satan was determined to prove that Jesus was not a true Man but just another "god" claiming to be a superman. If Jesus was truly God in the flesh, the game was over, so to speak! Satan had managed to bring sin into our race, but if this holy Being, Jesus, was a true Man, that would change the whole playing field.

Jesus' answer to Satan was, "Away with you, Satan! For it is written, 'You shall worship the LORD your God, and Him only you shall serve'" (Matthew 4:10 NKJV). And that meant that *Satan should be worshiping Jesus,* not telling Jesus to worship him.

The spirit of Antichrist tells us that we can be like God. We see this in Eden, in the Tower of Babel, in the present-day towers that assert economic superiority, and in efforts to rule over other nations and impose godless laws in opposition to God's Law.

Instead of following the Truth as revealed in Jesus, "science" is becoming a god. Whatever "science' says, that is what we are told to follow. The laboratories of OK "science" are seeking ways to "make man" after their own imaginings, called Artificial Intelligence. All this will come together when Satan's man enters the rebuilt temple in Jerusalem proclaiming himself to be God!

THE TIME OF JACOB'S TROUBLE

ALAS! FOR THAT DAY IS GREAT,
SO THAT NONE IS LIKE IT;
AND IT IS THE TIME OF JACOB'S TROUBLE,
BUT HE SHALL BE SAVED OUT OF IT.
"FOR IT SHALL COME TO PASS IN THAT DAY,"
SAYS THE LORD OF HOSTS,
"THAT I WILL BREAK HIS YOKE FROM YOUR
NECK,
AND WILL BURST YOUR BONDS;
FOREIGNERS SHALL NO MORE ENSLAVE
THEM.
BUT THEY SHALL SERVE THE LORD THEIR
GOD,
AND DAVID THEIR KING,
WHOM I WILL RAISE UP FOR THEM,
THEREFORE DO NOT FEAR, O MY SERVANT
JACOB," SAYS THE LORD,
"NOR BE DISMAYED, O ISRAEL;
FOR BEHOLD, I WILL SAVE YOU FROM AFAR,

AND YOUR SEED FROM THE LAND OF THEIR CAPTIVITY.
JACOB SHALL RETURN, HAVE REST AND BE QUIET,
AND NO ONE SHALL MAKE HIM AFRAID.
FOR I AM WITH YOU," SAYS THE LORD, "TO SAVE YOU;
THOUGH I MAKE A FULL END OF ALL THE NATIONS WHERE I HAVE SCATTERED YOU,
YET I WILL NOT MAKE A COMPLETE END OF YOU.
BUT I WILL CORRECT YOU IN JUSTICE,
AND WILL NOT LET YOU GO ALTOGETHER UNPUNISHED."

Jeremiah 30:7–11 NKJV

SATAN'S DESIRE TO DO AWAY WITH ISRAEL is revealed in the 12th chapter of Revelation. A woman, who is Israel, is in labor. A dragon wants to devour the child as soon as he is born. But the woman's child is caught up to God and His throne. The woman flees from the dragon. She goes into the wilderness to a place God prepared for her, where she is nourished for 1,260 days or 3 ½ years, the latter half of Daniel's 70th week.

Many Bible scholars believe that Israel's refuge will be in Petra. I have visited Petra. To reach the ancient red rock city, it is necessary to go through a deep and narrow rock canyon. When heavy rains occur, anything in that narrow passageway is swept away. Petra's topography appears to support the description given in Revelation:

> *The serpent poured water like a river out of his mouth after the woman so that he might cause her to be swept away with the flood. And the earth helped the woman and the earth opened its mouth and drank up the river which the dragon poured out of his mouth. And the dragon was enraged with the woman, and went off to make war with the rest of her offspring, who keep the commandment of God and hold to the testimony of Jesus.*
>
> Revelation 12:15–17 NASB

When Antichrist enters the Jewish temple and establishes himself as God, his true nature will be revealed. Jesus said of that time:

> *When you see the "abomination of desolation," spoken of by Daniel the prophet, standing in the holy place, then let those who are in Judea flee to the mountains. Let him who is on the housetop not go down to take anything out of his house. And let him who is in the field not go back to get his clothes. ...For then there will be great tribulation, such as has not been since the beginning of the world until this time, no, nor ever shall be. And unless those days were shortened, no flesh would be saved; but for the elect's sake those days will be shortened.*
>
> Matthew 24:15–18, 21–22 NKJV

At that time, God will send Israel His two witnesses who will proclaim the Truth to Israel (Revelation 11). Christians have long debated who they will be. Most agree that Elijah will be one as he is to appear before the coming of Messiah (Malachi 4:5). Further, Elijah did not die; he was caught up to heaven alive (2 Kings 2). Some believe the other witness will be Enoch because he also did not die (Genesis 5:24). Other Christian scholars believe the second witness will be Moses. He died, but God buried him (Deuteronomy 34:6). Moses is the only person we know that God buried. Jude 9 states that the archangel Michael, Israel's guardian, disputed with Satan about Moses' body. Why was Satan so concerned about Moses' body? Additionally, the signs that the two witnesses perform are similar to those that Moses and Elijah did in their day (Revelation 11:6). The two witnesses minister to Israel for half of Daniel's 70th week, or 3½ years.

In preparation for the Great Tribulation and the time of Jacob's Trouble, God puts His seal on 144,000 Jews from twelve tribes of Israel (Revelation 7:4-8). God's seal gives them special protection from powerful satanic activity. The persecution of Jews, Christians, and anyone who will not worship the Beast will be unimaginable during the second half of Daniel's 70th week. The 144,000 are select Jewish ministers of God. We see them again in Revelation 14 on Mount Zion with the Lamb. God gives them a very special place in His kingdom.

During the Great Tribulation and Jacob's Trouble, Satan is not the only one working his will. At the same time, the Lord God and His holy angels also will be very busy accomplishing great things on earth and in heaven.

GOD'S WAY AND MAN'S WAY

THE LORD CAME DOWN TO SEE THE CITY AND THE TOWER THAT THE PEOPLE HAD STARTED BUILDING. AND THE LORD SAID, "IF AS ONE PEOPLE ALL SHARING A COMMON LANGUAGE THEY HAVE BEGUN TO DO THIS, THEN NOTHING THEY PLAN TO DO WILL BE BEYOND THEM."

GENESIS 11:5–6 NET

After God created humankind, He desired that the human race be fruitful and multiply and fill the earth. He explicitly stated this after Adam's creation and again to Noah's descendants after the flood (Genesis 1:28 and 9:1).

God's way is through sovereign nationhood, not mass unification and a One World Order. He wants humanity to have the independence and freedom to reach out and find Him.

> *From one man he has made every nation of humanity to live all over the earth. He has given them the seasons of the year and the boundaries within which to live. He has done this so that they would look for God, somehow reach for him, and find him.*
>
> Acts 17:26–27 GW

Instead, human pride sought its own way. People congregated in one location and desired to build their own city and a tower reaching into the heavens, searching for knowledge apart from God, partaking of the Tree of the Knowledge of Good and Evil.

Godless society's efforts, from Babel to the Roman Empire to Hitler's Third Reich, have been to bring all nations together under a form of totalitarian government, seeking ways to enslave people and take away their God-given identity and freedom, dictating how one should think, speak, and act.

Godless humanity is still searching the heavens for knowledge from beings other than the Living God. The "spiritual hosts of wickedness in the heavenly places"

(Ephesians 6:12 NKJV) are only too glad to welcome such seekers.

Such a godless quest will ultimately end in the horrors of demonism, which will be rampant in the days before the return of Jesus Christ. Godless human quests have monstrous ends, both physically and spiritually.

In the past, the possibilities of alien life and UFOs were generally scoffed at. The Pentagon has now made some of its UFO files public, acknowledging that there have been manifestations of extraterrestrial beings. UFOs are now called Unidentified Aerial Phenomena, or UAPs.

The world is being conditioned to accept the existence of extraterrestrials, superbeings that may provide us with superior knowledge. (The 1982 movie *ET* introduced the concept of harmless and lovable extraterrestrials.)

King Solomon said there is "nothing new under the sun" (Ecclesiastes 1:9). The earth displays evidence of the existence of non-human activity on earth in past ages, such as the Great Pyramids of Egypt and England's chalk figures. Skeletons of giant beings buried in earth's past have been uncovered in various places. The Bible speaks of giants on the earth, the progeny of fallen angels and the daughters of Adam, huge beings who were neither angel nor human (Genesis 6:4).

The Book of Enoch (not in the canon of Biblical scripture but referred to in the Book of Jude) tells of such. Jude states,

> *Angels who did not keep their own domain, but abandoned their proper abode, He has kept in eternal bonds under darkness for the judgment of the great day, just as Sodom and Gomorrah and the cities around them, since they in the same way as these indulged in gross immorality and went after strange flesh, are exhibited as an example in undergoing the punishment of eternal fire.*
>
> Jude 1:6–7 NASB

Every life form has its own DNA. Since God made mankind in His own image and after His likeness, human DNA is sacred. Satan's fallen angels contaminated human DNA by copulating with the daughters of Adam. (Angels can take human form temporarily, but it does not make them true human beings.) Their progeny was neither human nor angel. They were giants and very violent. (Greek and Roman mythology may have its origins in such beings).

Israel was warned to not worship the sun, moon, and stars as the nations surrounding them did. "Take heed, lest you lift your eyes to heaven, and when you see the sun, the moon, and the stars, all the host of heaven, you feel driven to worship them and serve them" (Deuteronomy 4:19 NKJV).

The Apostle Paul acknowledges the nature of such worship when he warns the Corinthian Church regarding food that the Gentiles sacrificed to idols. "The things which the Gentiles sacrifice, they sacrifice to demons, and not to God" (1 Corinthians 10:20 NASB).

God said in Genesis 11:6 that nothing that humanity proposed to do would be impossible. Being made in God's image and after His likeness, humanity's potential is beyond our imagination. God's concern is not that He made the human race with such potential but that it might be used in the wrong way!

Apart from the righteousness of God, we are capable of unimaginable evil. Today, even many scientists fear what we may create in the laboratory or through technology. We have seen what gain of function research can do. Artificial Intelligence in the hands of evil people can become a living nightmare.*

* In 1946, C.S. Lewis wrote *That Hideous Strength: A Modern Fairy-Tale for Grown-Ups*, prophetic of what we are seeing today.

THE BEAST

THIS CALLS FOR WISDOM: LET THE ONE WHO HAS INSIGHT CALCULATE THE BEAST'S NUMBER, FOR IT IS MAN'S NUMBER, AND HIS NUMBER IS 666.

REVELATION 13:18 NET

THE PROPHECY OF DANIEL CHAPTER 7 presents the world empires as four beasts that come up out of the sea. The first is like a lion, the second a bear, and the third a leopard. The fourth beast is the most terrifying. Satan's man, the Antichrist, comes out of this beast as "a little horn."

The Beast that comes up out of the sea in Revelation 13 mirrors the characteristics of the four empires in Daniel's prophecy. "The beast which I saw was like a leopard, and his feet were like those of a bear, and his mouth like the mouth of a lion" (Revelation 13:2 NASB).

Both Daniel and Revelation present human civilization as bestial. Are we shocked by this simile? Not only is there "tooth and claw" in the world of wild animals, but human history drips with human blood. We like to think that civilization has progressed. Judeo-Christian law and ethics have brought about much good. But Hitler and the Holocaust came out of "Christian" society, and since 1973, the United States of America has killed over 63 million infant human lives through abortion.

The Beast has seven heads. There is much differing opinion about what the seven heads represent. We know that the head contains the brain that directs the body. One of the heads of the Beast appears to have been slain, but its fatal wound was healed (Revelation 13:3). Satan's false trinity (Satan, Antichrist, and False Prophet) also has a "death and resurrection!"

The Beast has ten horns, and on the ten horns are ten crowns. Crowns speak of kingdoms. Daniel describes the fourth beast like this:

> *Behold, a fourth beast, dreadful and terrifying and extremely strong; and it had large teeth. It devoured and crushed and trampled down the remainder with its feet; and it was different from all the beasts that were before it, and it had ten horns. ... Behold, another horn, a little one, came up among them, and three of the first horns were pulled out by the roots before it; and behold, this*

horn possessed eyes like the eyes of a man and a mouth uttering great boasts.

Daniel 7:7–8 NASB

The "little horn" is Satan's man, the Antichrist. He has eyes like a human, but what comes out of his mouth is devilish.

Then, another beast rises from the earth. Satan has no power over the earth without human consent and participation. So out of the earth, which represents the human race, rises the second beast that has two horns like a lamb but speaks like a dragon (Revelation 13:11).

The second beast of Satan's unholy trinity, the False Prophet, corresponds to the third Person of the Holy Trinity, the Holy Spirit. Jesus said of the Holy Spirit, "He will glorify Me, for He will take of what is Mine and declare it to you" (John 16:14 NKJV). The False Prophet will cause the world to worship the first beast and even make an image of the first beast that will be given supernatural powers.

He performed momentous signs, even making fire come down from heaven to earth in front of people and, by the signs he was permitted to perform on behalf of the beast, he deceived those who live on the earth. He told those who live on the earth to make an image to the beast who had been wounded by the sword, but still lived. The second beast was empowered to give

> *life to the image of the first beast so that it could speak, and could cause all those who did not worship the image of the beast to be killed.*
>
> Revelation 13:12–15 NET

It seems reasonable to wonder if the image of the Beast will be a form of Artificial Intelligence.

It is important to note that the first beast's fatal wound is healed. At the heart of Christianity is the death and resurrection of Jesus Christ. Satan's "resurrection" will greatly impact those who witness it. "One of the beast's heads appeared to have been killed, but the lethal wound had been healed. And the whole world followed the beast in amazement" (Revelation 13:3 NET).

The Satanic trinity, in all aspects, is called a *beast*. A beast is not human. True humanity is found in the Lord Jesus Christ – He is righteous, holy, loving, does good, is self-sacrificing, and life-giving.

The Beast will appear human, with eyes like a man's, but its nature will be Satanic. It speaks like a dragon. Those who refuse to worship the Beast and its image and refuse to take its Mark will be persecuted, starved, hounded, imprisoned and slain.

The number of the Beast is 666: "it is the number of a man" (Revelation 13:18 NKJV). It is a trinity of sixes, mimicking the Holy Trinity. The number 7 represents completion or perfection. Seven is God's number. The difference between 6 and 7, one number, is infinite. The missing number, or link, is God's Life. Humanity was created to express all the fullness of God (Ephesians 3:19). The difference between a human being who shares in the Life of God and one who shares in the Satanic trinity is beyond our imagination.

No matter how much power a person gains, the end is death if separated from the Life of God. Power without the Life and holiness of God becomes monstrous!

Revelation also states that those who worship the Beast, who are linked with its identity through its Mark, are worshiping the Dragon, or Satan, who gives power to the Beast (Revelation 13:2). When one is born of the Holy Spirit, that person is a new creation in God. (2 Corinthians 5:17). When one takes the Mark of the Beast, that person is accepting a satanic identity.

When the Lord God breathed the breath of life into Adam's nostrils, Adam became a living soul (Genesis 2:7). "Lostness" is losing your human soul. Jesus said, "What will it profit a man if he gains the whole world, and loses his own soul? Or what will a man give in exchange for his soul" (Mark 8:36-37 NKJV). Once you lose your soul, you lose something of your God-given identity which cannot be recovered. That is true lostness, a loss to both yourself and God.

The message of the Beast is prideful, blasphemous, anti-God and anti-Christ, and it wars against the saints. "If anyone is meant for captivity, into captivity he will go. If anyone is to be killed by the sword, then by the sword he must be killed. This requires steadfast endurance and faith from the saints" (Revelation 13:10 NET).

The Antichrist's and False Prophet's end is revealed in Revelation 19:20. They are cast into the Lake of Fire. But Satan, the dragon, the serpent of old, the devil, is chained, temporarily, until the end of the Millennium (Revelation 20:2).

THE FINAL JUDGMENTS

IMMEDIATELY AFTER THE TRIBULATION OF THOSE DAYS THE SUN WILL BE DARKENED, AND THE MOON WILL NOT GIVE ITS LIGHT; THE STARS WILL FALL FROM HEAVEN, AND THE POWERS OF THE HEAVENS WILL BE SHAKEN.

MATTHEW 24:29 NKJV

We cannot imagine the horrible events that will take place under the rule of the Antichrist. We know what happened under Hitler's Third Reich. It will be much worse under the Antichrist when Satan is unrestrained.

The whole world will be involved. As Jesus said, "There will be a great tribulation such as has not occurred since the beginning of the world until now, nor ever shall" (Matthew 24:21 NASB). It will be so horrendous that even the heavens will be shaken. Darkness will prevail.

I looked when He broke the sixth seal, and there was a great earthquake; and the sun became black as sackcloth made of hair, and the whole moon became like blood; and the stars of the sky fell to the earth, as a fig tree casts its unripe figs when shaken by the great wind. The sky was split apart like a scroll when it is rolled up, and every mountain and island were moved out of their places.

Revelation 6:12–14 NASB

The fourth angel sounded, and a third of the sun and a third of the moon and a third of the stars were struck, so that a third of them would be darkened and the day would not shine for a third of it, and the night in the same way.

Revelation 8:12 NASB

Then the fifth angel poured out his bowl on the throne of the beast so that darkness covered his kingdom, and people began to bite their tongues because of their pain. They blasphemed the God of heaven because of their sufferings and because of their sores, but nevertheless they still refused to repent of their deeds.

Revelation 16:8–10 NET

The earth quakes,
The heavens tremble,
The sun and the moon grow dark
And the stars lose their brightness.

Joel 2:10

As the Light of the World is denied and blasphemed, spiritual and physical darkness descend. God's first words were, "Let there be light." Sinful humankind brings darkness upon itself.

But through the darkness and great suffering, God does not abandon humanity. He uses an angel to proclaim an "eternal gospel" (Revelation 14:6-7). Probably, at that point, travel will be impossible. So God uses His angels to proclaim His word. He even does so today where His word is not available. There are many testimonies of such.

The eternal gospel is to worship God and know that He is the One who has created all that exists. This basic truth is what will go out into the whole universe for all eternity. The first of the Ten Commandments is: "You shall have no other gods before Me" (Exodus 20:3). That is, truly, an eternal gospel! Another angel warns those who are tempted to worship the Beast and his image and receive the mark of his name. The description of their judgment is the most severe of all of God's judgments (Revelation 14:9-11).

In the face of all of this, there is the exhortation to those who believe in God: "This requires the steadfast endurance of the saints – those who obey God's commandments and hold to their faith in Jesus" (Revelation 14:12 NET).

In all times and circumstances, may we be able to sing the song:

He is Lord, He is Lord !
He is risen from the dead, and He is Lord!
Every knee shall bow and every tongue confess
That Jesus Christ is Lord.

ARMAGEDDON

I SAW COMING OUT OF THE MOUTH OF THE DRAGON AND OUT OF THE MOUTH OF THE BEAST AND OUT OF THE MOUTH OF THE FALSE PROPHET, THREE UNCLEAN SPIRITS LIKE FROGS; FOR THEY ARE SPIRITS OF DEMONS, PERFORMING SIGNS, WHICH GO OUT TO THE KINGS OF THE WHOLE WORLD, TO GATHER THEM TOGETHER FOR THE WAR OF THE GREAT DAY OF GOD, THE ALMIGHTY. ... AND THEY GATHERED THEM TOGETHER TO THE PLACE WHICH IN HEBREW IS CALLED HAR–MAGEDON.

REVELATION 16:13–14, 16 NASB

ALMOST EVERYONE HAS HEARD of the Battle of Armageddon. It brings to mind thoughts of the end and a decisive world battle, which it is. It is the end of Satan's rule on earth.

Satan was once a high and powerful angel, and his power on earth is a fact. He had access to the Garden of Eden, and Jesus called him "the prince of this world" (John 14:30 KJV). Just because Satan fell does not mean he doesn't have a position of power. God does not do things by waving a wand or making arbitrary declarations. He respects the order He established.

This order applies to us also. God has given us the freedom to choose both good and evil, and the consequences of our choices are real!

> *Do not be deceived, God is not mocked; for whatever a man sows, that he will also reap. For he who sows to his flesh will of the flesh reap corruption, but he who sows to the Spirit will of the Spirit reap everlasting life. And let us not grow weary while doing good, for in due season we shall reap if we do not lose heart.*
>
> Galatians 6:7–9 NKJV

Armageddon means "hill of Megiddo." Wicked Ahab, king of the northern ten tribes of Israel, had a fortress there named Megiddo overlooking the plain of Jezreel, which means "place of battles." It is said that when Napoleon viewed the plain of Jezreel, he saw it as the world's battlefield, a place where the world's armies could maneuver.

When the sixth bowl is poured out, three demonic spirits from the Satanic trinity will influence the leaders of the world, who will gather together to war against the Lord. "They are spirits of demons, performing signs, which go out to the kings of the whole world, to gather them together for the war of the great day of God, the Almighty" (Revelation 16:14 NASB).

The demonic spirits are depicted as frogs. A frog catches its prey with its tongue. We tell lies with our tongue. The world's leaders will be deceived by the unholy trinity's lies and drawn into Satan's net.

The Euphrates River will dry up, facilitating the invasion of Israel by armies from the East (Revelation 16:12). The fact that all the leaders of the world are led to fight Israel shows the power of the false trinity over the world. It is Satan's last attempt to utterly destroy Israel. Every leader on earth will join in fighting Israel.

Why have the Jews and Israel been so hated and persecuted? Because the world is under the influence of the "prince of this world," Satan, who hates the nation of Israel and the Jews from whom God chose to bring forth His Son into the world.

It is reasonable to ask: "How can Satan think that he can defeat Almighty God?" But sin is not reasonable. Sin says, "I will do what I want to do regardless of the consequences." The pride and willfulness of sin are irrational. Ernest William Henley's poem "Invictus" expresses the spirit of pride and rebellion so well:

Out of the night that covers me,
Black as the Pit from pole to pole,
I thank whatever gods may be
For my unconquerable soul.
In the fell clutch of circumstance
I have not winced or cried aloud.
Under the bludgeonings of chance
My head is bloody, but unbowed.
Beyond this place of wrath and tears
Looms but the Horror of the shade,
And yet the menace of the years
Finds, and shall find, me unafraid.
It matters not how strait the gate,
How charged with punishments the scroll,
I am the master of my fate:
I am the captain of my soul.

1875

Satan once was very high and magnificent, but pride brought him low.

How you are fallen from heaven,
O Lucifer, son of the morning!
How you are cut down to the ground,
You who weakened the nations!
For you have said in your heart:
"I will ascend into heaven,
I will exalt my throne above the stars of God,
I will also sit on the mount of the congregation

On the farthest sides of the north;
I will ascend above heights of the clouds,
I will be like the Most High."

Isaiah 14:12–14 NKJV

In June 1967, Israel fought the Six-Day War. That war lasted only six days, but it gave Jerusalem and the Temple Mount back to the Jews. However, politics compromised Israel's control over Jerusalem and the Temple Mount, and Jerusalem is still trodden down by the Gentiles, and it will be until the Battle of Armageddon. In that day, God will fight for Israel. Armageddon will be God's Seventh-Day War!

Then the LORD will go forth and fight against those nations, as when He fights on a day of battle. In that day his feet will stand on the Mount of Olives, which is in front of Jerusalem on the east; and the Mount of Olives will be split in its middle from east to west by a very large valley, so that half of the mountain will move toward the north and the other half toward the south. ... Then the LORD, my God, will come, and all the holy ones with Him!

Zechariah 14:3–5 NASB

I saw heaven opened, and behold a white horse, and He who sat upon it is called Faithful and True, and in righteousness He judges and wages war. His eyes are a flame of fire, and on His head are many diadems; and He has a name written on Him which no one knows except Himself. He is clothed with a robe dipped in blood, and His name is called The Word of God. And the armies which are in heaven, clothed in fine linen, white and clean, were following Him on white horses.

Revelation 19:11–14 NASB

He has a name that only He knows. God is infinite. Even those who share His Life will never be able to know the infinity of God. Only the Son, who is the expression of the infinite God, can fathom all that God is. But those who love God and seek after Him have begun an infinite, glorious journey.

"From His mouth comes a sharp sword, so that with it He may strike down the nations" (Revelation 19:15 NASB). God's weapon against the nations that come against Him is a sharp sword, and it comes from His mouth. The sword of God's Spirit is His Word (Ephesians 6:17). The Lord Jesus Christ is the Word of God. God wins the Battle of Armageddon by His Word, His only begotten Son! Jesus is the Truth of God. The Lie cannot stand before the Truth.

Martin Luther's great hymn, "A Mighty Fortress Is Our God," expresses it well:

And though this world, with devils filled,
should threaten to undo us,
we will not fear, for God hath willed
His truth to triumph through us.

The Prince of Darkness grim,
we tremble not for him;
his rage we can endure,
for lo, his doom is sure;
one little word shall fell him.

That Word above all earthly powers,
no thanks to them, abideth;
the Spirit and the gifts are ours,
thru Him who with us sideth.

Let goods and kindred go,
this mortal life also;
the body they may kill;
God's truth abideth still;
His kingdom is forever.

c. 1529

The Battle of Armageddon ends the evil rule of Satan and begins the rule of the Messiah, the Lord Jesus Christ, from Jerusalem. Satan is temporarily cast into his own prison, the abyss, and the Millennium begins.

THE MILLENNIUM

THE NURSING CHILD WILL PLAY BY THE HOLE OF THE COBRA, AND THE WEANED CHILD WILL PUT HIS HAND ON THE VIPER'S DEN.

ISAIAH 11:9 NASB

THE THOUSAND-YEAR REIGN OF CHRIST is mentioned five times in Revelation 20. After Satan is bound and locked up, God's order is established, and human society will no longer be under the influence of Satanic deceit.

One might ask, "Why does it end? Isn't this the kind of world that we have always wanted? Why only a thousand years?" What is the purpose of the Millennium?

At the end of the thousand years, Satan is released from his prison. Look what happens. He again deceives the nations and gathers an army. Their number will be like "the sand of the seashore." Again, the world's armies go against Jerusalem (Revelation 20:7-9). Gog and Magog are named. Magog is the name of the son of Jafeth, Noah's son, from whom the gentile nations come.

All those years, the nations looked to Jerusalem and followed the Law of God. Yet again, Satan deceives humanity and causes the nations to once again rebel against God. The Law is not the answer! Control from the outside does not change the inside. Listen to the prophet Micah.

> *In the future the LORD's Temple Mount will be the most important mountain of all;*
> *it will be more prominent than other hills.*
> *People will stream to it.*
> *Many nations will come, saying,*
> *"Come on! Let's go up to the LORD's mountain,*
> *to the temple of Jacob's God,*
> *so he can teach us his commands*
> *and we can live by his laws."*
> *For Zion will be the source of instruction;*
> *The LORD's teachings will proceed from Jerusalem,*
> *He will arbitrate between many peoples*
> *and settle disputes between many distant nations.*
> *They will beat their swords into plowshares,*
> *and their spears into pruning hooks.*
> *Nations will not use weapons against other nations,*

and they will no longer train for war.
Each will sit under his own grapevine
or under his own fig tree without any fear.
The LORD who commands armies has decreed it.
Though all the nations follow their respective gods,
we will follow the LORD our God forever.

Micah 4:1–5 NET

The unregenerate human heart can obey the law yet serve its own gods. It says: "Let the reverend, pastor, or priest tell me how to live, but I can still do my own thing – as long as it isn't too bad. I don't need to get *that* close to God. I can conform to the norm and still enjoy my own life. As long as I can have my own grapevine, sit under my own fig tree, live in peace, be healthy and live a long life – what more could a person want?"

But there is so much more that God wants for us. He wants to give us His own Life, which He gave to the world in His Son. He is waiting for each one of us.

Therefore the LORD longs to be gracious to you,
And therefore He waits on high to have compassion on you.
For the LORD is a God of justice;
How blessed are all those who long for Him.

Isaiah 30:18 NASB

Jesus said, "You are unwilling to come to Me so that you may have life" (John 5:40 NASB). When Jesus told His followers that manna was not enough, that they must partake of His flesh and blood (His flesh speaks of His holy humanity, and His blood speaks of His divine Life), the majority of those following Him said, "This is a difficult saying! Who can understand it?" (John 6:60 NET).

Just go to church and try to be good. Isn't that enough? No, it isn't. We need the holy Life of God, which can never be deceived nor has any inclination to sin. When Jesus said that Satan has nothing in Him, He was testifying to His holy humanity. He insisted we *must* be born again from above (John 3:7).

Just as the Great Tribulation and its aftermath will be an eternal lesson exposing the horror of sin and its end, the Millennium will show that the Law is not enough to change a person's heart. We need Life!

THE GREAT WHITE THRONE

AND I SAW THE DEAD, THE GREAT AND THE SMALL, STANDING BEFORE THE THRONE AND THE BOOKS WERE OPENED; AND ANOTHER BOOK WAS OPENED, WHICH IS THE BOOK OF LIFE; AND THE DEAD WERE JUDGED FROM THE THINGS WHICH WERE WRITTEN IN THE BOOKS, ACCORDING TO THEIR DEEDS. AND THE SEA GAVE UP THE DEAD WHICH WERE IN IT, AND DEATH AND HADES GAVE UP THE DEAD WHICH WERE IN THEM; AND THEY WERE JUDGED, EVERY ONE OF THEM ACCORDING TO THEIR DEEDS. THEN DEATH AND HADES WERE THROWN INTO THE LAKE OF FIRE. THIS IS THE SECOND DEATH, THE LAKE OF FIRE. AND IF ANYONE'S NAME WAS NOT FOUND WRITTEN IN THE BOOK OF LIFE, HE WAS THROWN INTO THE LAKE OF FIRE.

Revelation 20:12–15 NASB

THE GREAT WHITE THRONE JUDGMENT takes place after the Millennium. Heaven and earth have *fled* from the presence of the One seated on the throne.

There was no longer any place found for the old heaven and earth. They had served their purpose. There is to be a new heaven and earth in which righteousness dwells (2 Peter 3:13).

The first resurrection will already have taken place. Those who share in the first resurrection include the Church (1 Thessalonians 4:16-17), “His elect from the four winds, from one end of heaven to the other” (Matthew 24:31 NET), and “the souls of those who had been beheaded because of the testimony about Jesus and because of the word of God. These had not worshipped the beast or his image and had refused to receive his mark on their forehead or hand” (Revelation 20:4 NET).

The rest of the dead are not raised until the thousand years are completed. They have come out of the sea, Death and Hades. God knows the distinctions.

They appear before the Great White Throne judgment. Their judgment is based on testimony to their deeds recorded in books. There also is the Book of Life, which bears testimony to the holy life of Jesus Christ, who will be present because He will be doing the judging. The

Father has turned over all judgment to the Son. Jesus explains:

> *He gave Him authority to execute judgment, because He is the Son of Man. ... An hour is coming, in which all who are in the tombs will hear His voice, and will come forth; those who did the good deeds to a resurrection of life, those who committed the evil deeds to a resurrection of judgment.*
>
> John 5:27–29 NASB

As the Lamb of God is lifted up before their gaze and they see the meaning of the Cross, those who rejected Him and those who sinned against the Truth that He is will weep and gnash their teeth. The anger will not be at God but at themselves.

There will be no argument. Jesus said, "I, when I am lifted up from the earth, will draw all people to myself" (John 12:32 NET).

Will all who appear before the Great White Throne suffer the same judgment? If that were so, there would not be any need for the testimony written in the books.

In Romans chapter 2, the Apostle Paul explains the meaning of the true Law as it applies to God's judgment:

> *It is not the hearers of the Law who are just before God, but the doers of the Law will be*

> *justified. For when Gentiles who do not have the Law do instinctively the things of the Law, these, not having the Law, are a law to themselves, in that they show the work of the Law written in their hearts, their conscience bearing witness and their thoughts alternately accusing or else defending them, on the day when, according to my gospel, God will judge the secrets of men through Christ Jesus.*
>
> Romans 2:13–16 NASB

Will all the dead who appear before the Great White Throne experience the second death, the Lake of Fire? The Lord alone knows those who are written in the Book of Life. I do know that the Judge at the Great White Throne is the Lamb of God who takes away the sin of the world.

THE LAKE OF FIRE

BLESSED AND HOLY IS THE ONE WHO HAS A PART IN THE FIRST RESURRECTION; OVER THESE THE SECOND DEATH HAS NO POWER.

REVELATION 20:6 NASB

THE LAKE OF FIRE IS THE SECOND DEATH. We all must experience the First Death. After Eve and Adam disobeyed the Lord, death set in. Death results from separation from the life of God. Physical death is caused by spiritual death. Death is not part of life. Death is the antithesis of life.

Aging is the process of dying. But while we suffer aging, illness and dying, we have the opportunity to receive the life of the Lord Jesus Christ, who rose from the dead in a glorified body that can never die. Thus, physical death for someone who has the Life of God's Son is not the same as the death of someone who is spiritually dead.

Jesus told Martha at the death of her brother Lazarus, "I am the resurrection and the life; he who believes in Me will live even if he dies, and everyone who lives and believes in Me will never die" (John 11:25-26 NASB).

Our bodies die because they have the seed of corruption in them. After Adam and Eve sinned, God guarded access to the Tree of Life so that sinful flesh might not live forever (Genesis 3:22-24). What a horrible thought - eternal sin!

The root of physical death is found in a person's spirit. Uncleanness of the spirit must be dealt with even after the sinful body has died. For this, the Second Death is necessary. Nothing unclean can live in God's Universe.

Jesus said, "I have come to cast fire upon the earth; and how I wish it were already kindled! But I have a baptism to undergo, and how distressed I am until it is accomplished" (Luke 12:49-50 NASB). His distress came from His longing for our deliverance from sin and death, and He knew that the process would bring about much suffering, not just for Him but for us. In Gethsemane, the burden He bore for us would have killed Him had not angels come and ministered to Him.

It is Jesus who kindles the fire of God! By refusing to leave us and making His holy humanity a part of our race, He kindled the fire that takes place when God's holiness embraces sinful humanity.

The Holy Spirit descended upon Jesus at His baptism as a dove. When the Holy Spirit came upon the believers at Pentecost, it was not as a dove of peace but as tongues of fire.

"For the Lord your God is a consuming fire; he is a jealous God" (Deuteronomy 4:24 NET). Righteous jealousy is not envy. God's jealous love saves us from all that would destroy us. "For the wrath of God is revealed from heaven against all ungodliness and unrighteousness of people who suppress the truth by their unrighteousness" (Romans 1:18 NET). God's wrath preserves the truth. God's wrath is good. All that God does is for our good.

The Apostle Paul warns the Corinthian church of the possibility that their deeds will suffer the judgment of God's fire. "If someone's work is burned up, he will suffer loss. He himself will be saved, but only as through fire" (1 Corinthians 3:15 NET). God's fire burns up garbage, removing all that is a hindrance to life and godliness. All imperfection and corruption are to be eliminated from God's creation through His cleansing, purifying fire.

How the Lake Of Fire will accomplish this purification, we do not know. But God does. Each case will be different. However, if there is a first death and a first resurrection, it is reasonable to expect a second resurrection after the second death. But the secret things belong to the Lord our God (Deuteronomy 29:29).

Jesus' words about judgment are figurative and metaphorical, symbolic of that which we cannot imagine. Only God knows the true nature of our potential loss.

The Lake of Fire is not a place where God discards those whom He has created to be tortured or annihilated. It is a place where everything that would destroy and hurt will be consumed, a place of purification where what can be saved will be saved. God's salvage operation is the best! There will be no dungeons or torture chambers in God's universe!

NEW HEAVENS AND A NEW EARTH

ACCORDING TO HIS PROMISE WE ARE LOOKING FOR NEW HEAVENS AND A NEW EARTH, IN WHICH RIGHTEOUSNESS DWELLS.

2 PETER 3:13 NASB

THE PROMISE OF NEW HEAVENS AND A NEW EARTH is found in Isaiah 65:17: "Behold, I create new heavens and a new earth; and the former things will not be remembered or come to mind." The wonder and joy of God's Masterpiece will outweigh all previous suffering – Life, nothing but Life and all the beauty, joy, and wonder that it brings!

Jesus said, "Whenever a woman is in labor she has pain, because her hour has come; but when she gives birth to the child, she no longer remembers the anguish because of the joy that a child has been born into the world" (John 16:21 NASB).

"Then I saw a new heaven and a new earth, for the first heaven and earth had ceased to exist, and the sea existed no more" (Revelation 21:1 NET). In the new earth, all will be pure. There will be no need for the salty seas because there will be no fiery abyss. There will be no erupting volcanoes, earthquakes, hurricanes, or wildfires. Nature will be at peace.

"And the one seated on the throne said: 'Look! I am making all things new! ... It is done! I am the Alpha and the Omega, the beginning and the end'" (Revelation 21:5, 6 NET). Satan will be cast into the Lake of Fire. Death and Hell are also cast into the Lake of Fire (Revelation 20:10, 14). Satan, Death, and Hell are neither the beginning nor the end.*

Heaven and earth will undergo transfiguration through fire. "The present heavens and earth are being reserved for fire, kept for the day of judgment" (2 Peter 3:7 NASB).

---

* The word "forever" is a misleading English translation of the Hebrew "olam" and Greek "aeon," which means a period of time or an age. "Forever and ever" means ages of ages.

The fire that the Lord Jesus kindled on earth by His Presence will transfigure both earth and heaven.

After earth and heaven are cleansed and purified, there will be a perfect union of both. The New Jerusalem will descend from heaven (Revelation 21:10). "Look! The residence of God is among human beings. He will live among them, and they will be his people, and God himself will be with them" (Revelation 21:3 NET).

> *Mercy and truth are met together;*
> *Righteousness and peace have kissed each other.*
> *Truth shall spring out of the earth;*
> *And righteousness shall look down from heaven.*
>
> Psalm 85:10–11 KJV

THE COMING OF THE SON OF MAN

FOR JUST LIKE THE LIGHTNING, WHEN IT FLASHES OUT OF ONE PART OF THE SKY, SHINES TO THE OTHER PART OF THE SKY, SO WILL THE SON OF MAN BE IN HIS DAY.

LUKE 17:24 NASB

IN HIS OLIVET DISCOURSE, Jesus spoke of the sign of the Son of Man appearing in heaven. What is the sign? We find a possible answer in Daniel's prophecy.

During Jesus' trial, the high priest asked Him if He was the Christ, the Son of the Blessed One. Jesus answered, "I am, and you will see the Son of Man sitting at the right hand of Power and coming with the clouds of heaven"

(Mark 14:61-62 NET). At that point, the high priest accused Jesus of blasphemy.

The authorities knew Jesus was proclaiming His coming as the fulfillment of Daniel's prophecy – the Son of Man seated at the right hand of Power and coming with the clouds of heaven!

> *Behold, with the clouds of heaven*
> *One like a Son of Man was coming,*
> *And He came up to the Ancient of Days*
> *And was presented before Him.*
> *And to Him was given dominion,*
> *Glory and a kingdom,*
> *That all the peoples, nations and men of every language*
> *Might serve Him.*
> *His dominion is an everlasting dominion*
> *Which will not pass away;*
> *And His kingdom is one*
> *Which will not be destroyed.*
>
> Daniel 7:13–14 NASB

As the old order is judged, the heavens will open up, be rolled back like a scroll, and the earth will receive its true King.

Jesus said that His coming will be as lightning which lights up the sky from east to west (see this chapter's opening quotation from Luke). The whole world will see the coming of the Son of Man.

In conjunction with the coming of the Son of Man, the saints will be gathered from one end of heaven to the other.

> *They will see the Son of Man arriving on the clouds of heaven with power and great glory. And he will send his angels with a loud trumpet blast, and they will gather his elect from the four winds, from one end of heaven to the other.*
>
> Matthew 24:30–31 NET

Those of the faithful still living on earth will also be taken. "Then there will be two men in the field; one will be taken and one left. There will be two women grinding grain with a mill; one will be taken and one left" (Matthew 24:40-41 NET). They join the faithful from the four winds of heaven to be with the Lord when He returns.

PARABLE OF THE TEN VIRGINS

YOU, TOO, MUST BE READY BECAUSE THE SON OF MAN WILL RETURN WHEN YOU LEAST EXPECT HIM.

MATTHEW 24:44 GW

IN ALL THREE GOSPELS, Matthew, Mark, and Luke, the Olivet Discourse ends with a warning to be alert and ready for His return at all times. It is not by accident that Matthew's gospel gives us the parable of the Ten Virgins following the Olivet Discourse.

In the parable, the virgins represent the Church, and the oil speaks of the Holy Spirit. The Bridegroom represents the Lord Jesus. The virgins are gathered to meet the

Bridegroom. All ten have lamps burning, but only half of them have extra oil. The Bridegroom is delayed and doesn't come when they expect Him. The half that is not prepared with extra oil is unable to meet the Bridegroom because their lamps go out. Without light, they cannot find their way through the darkness to meet the Bridegroom.

After the door to His Presence is shut, the Bridegroom tells those who seek to enter later that He does not know them. Religion, or religious knowledge, is not enough. We may know all *about* people – their age, where they live, where they went to school, what work they do – and still we may not really know them.

Jesus warned that the deceptions of the last days will be so great that even the elect may be deceived. Without the protection and strength that only God can give, the deceptions of the Antichrist and the Beast will be overpowering. But, as Jesus tells us, the one who endures to the end will be saved (Matthew 24:13).

John 21 is the account of Jesus' meeting with His disciples by the Sea of Galilee after His resurrection. He had enabled them to catch a huge haul of fish. Jesus asked Peter, who had denied Him, "Do you love me more than these?" Perhaps Jesus was referring to the fish that Peter had just taken the time to count! But we all know what our own "these" are.

The deciding factor is how much we love and want the Lord. We get as much of God as we want. "Do you love me?" He asks. His next question is, "How much?"

Jesus warns,

> *Be on your guard so that your hearts are not weighed down with dissipation and drunkenness and the worries of this life, and that day close down upon you suddenly like a trap. For it will overtake all who live on the face of the whole earth. But stay alert at all times, praying that you may have strength to escape all these things that must happen, and to stand before the Son of Man.*
>
> Luke 21:34–36 NET

The parable of the Ten Virgins is a warning to the earthly Church. It is shocking that only five of the ten virgins, 50 percent, were ready. Jesus tells us to stay alert and pray that we might have the strength to escape the judgments that precede His return.

Jesus said the days before His return would be like "the days of Noah" (Matthew 24:37). Some prophetic scholars believe that there will be those who do escape "all these things that must happen" by being snatched away before the "days of Noah," as Enoch was.

Enoch was Noah's great-grandfather. Enoch had the testimony of having walked with God. "Enoch walked with God, and then he disappeared because God took him away" (Genesis 5:24 NET).

CONCLUSION

As long as we are in this world, we are here for "such a time as this." As we see the world and current events through the eyes of the One who is its Revelation, we will know how to take our place in our time.

The airwaves are full of "prophecies" that too often serve to excite and mislead. We must not live by bread alone but by every word of God. The Lord Jesus Christ is the Word of God. We must learn of Him and know Him in order to understand His prophetic word.

Our salvation lies not in being able to fit end time events into a neat order. Such a task can easily lead to pride. We need to understand the events of our time through the knowledge of our Savior and His ways. Then we can better understand the meaning behind the events.

As we face the approaching darkness, may we allow Him to trim our lamps and provide enough oil to see the path that leads to Him. Only the Light of His Life can enable us to faithfully stand in whatever time we live and find His Way when He calls us to meet Him.

About the Author

Rosemary Hyslop

Rosemary Hyslop decided to follow the Lord Jesus Christ as a teenager. She had access to the excellent library of her father, James Hyslop, who was a learned teacher of the Word. Inspired by her father's understanding and teaching of the Person of Christ, she continued to study the Bible in depth, as well as study to be a nurse. She received her Bachelor's in nursing, hoping to use her medical knowledge as a Christian missionary. She worked in a mission hospital in the Holy Land for only one year, returning home due to an illness in her family that required her care.

Believing that her mission was not abroad but at home, Rosemary used her nursing skills to care for her family while continuing her biblical studies. Many years later, she moved from her home in east central Ohio to a Christian community in north central Florida, where she has lived for almost two decades.

Rosemary has been writing on biblical subjects for almost twelve years, posting her studies on her web page, jesusatoninglife.com. She has previously published *God's Humanity: The Shocking Wonder of the Incarnation, The Atonement: Punishment or Person?,* and a book of poetry by her late sister Elsie Lewis Eastman, *The Dance.*

Rosemary shares what she sees in the Word, hoping others may deepen their understanding of the Christian life. Passionate about the "greatness of salvation" (Hebrews 2:3) found only in the Lord Jesus Christ, she earnestly believes that the Church must not only grow outward but upward (Hebrews 6:1).

More from Rosemary Hyslop

Available in paperback and as eBooks on Amazon

Also Available:

Available in paperback on Amazon

For more inspirational reading,
please visit Rosemary Hyslop's website:

JesusAtoningLife.com

www.ingramcontent.com/pod-product-compliance
Lightning Source LLC
LaVergne TN
LVHW010608160826
845677LV00013B/3315

* 9 7 9 8 9 8 6 3 5 3 3 5 7 *